Killer Whales

Leo Statts

abdopublishing.com

Published by Abdo Zoom™, PO Box 398166, Minneapolis, Minnesota 55439. Copyright © 2017 by Abdo Consulting Group, Inc. International copyrights reserved in all countries. No part of this book may be reproduced in any form without written permission from the publisher. Abdo Zoom™ is a trademark and logo of Abdo Consulting Group, Inc.

Printed in the United States of America, North Mankato, Minnesota
092016
012017

THIS BOOK CONTAINS RECYCLED MATERIALS

Cover Photo: iStockphoto
Interior Photos: Mike Price/Shutterstock Images, 1; Shutterstock Images, 4–5, 7; Evgeniya Lazareva/iStockphoto, 5; Tomasz Szymanski/iStockphoto, 6; Dave Riganelli/iStockphoto, 8; Chris Boswell/iStockphoto, 10–11; Red Line Editorial, 11, 20 (left), 20 (right), 21 (left), 21 (right); Paul Nicklen/National Geographic Creative, 12–13; Pablo Cersosimo/Robert Harding/Glow Images, 14; iStockphoto, 15, 18–19; Monika Wieland/Shutterstock Images, 16, 17

Editor: Brienna Rossiter
Series Designer: Madeline Berger
Art Direction: Dorothy Toth

Publisher's Cataloging-in-Publication Data
Names: Statts, Leo, author.
Title: Killer whales / by Leo Statts.
Description: Minneapolis, MN : Abdo Zoom, 2017. | Series: Ocean animals | Includes bibliographical references and index.
Identifiers: LCCN 2016948672 | ISBN 9781680799125 (lib. bdg.) | ISBN 9781624024986 (ebook) | ISBN 9781624025549 (Read-to-me ebook)
Subjects: LCSH: Killer whale--Juvenile literature.
Classification: DDC 599.5/6--dc23
LC record available at http://lccn.loc.gov/2016948672

Table of Contents

Killer Whales

Killer whales are also called orcas.
Their backs are black.
They have white on their bellies.

Under their tails is white, too.

A killer whale has huge, rounded flippers.

Its skin is smooth.
It has a tall fin on its back.

Killer whales have a special body part called a **melon**. It is inside their heads.

The melon sends
out clicking sounds.
The sounds help the
whales sense what
is around them.

Killer whales live in oceans around the world. They swim in groups called **pods**.

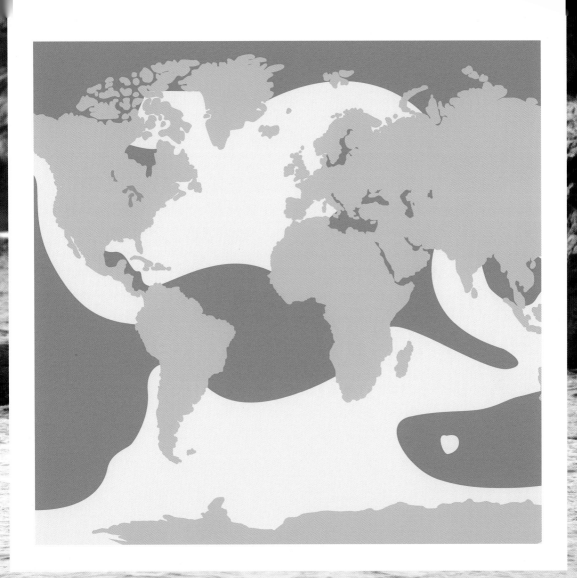

Where killer whales live

Killer whales often stay near shore.

But they **migrate**, too.
They can travel long distances.

Killer whales eat fish.
They also eat seals
and sea lions.

Their curved teeth hold
tightly on to **prey**.

Life Cycle

Killer whales have live babies.

Calves stay with their mothers for one to two years.

Male killer whales
can live 60 years.

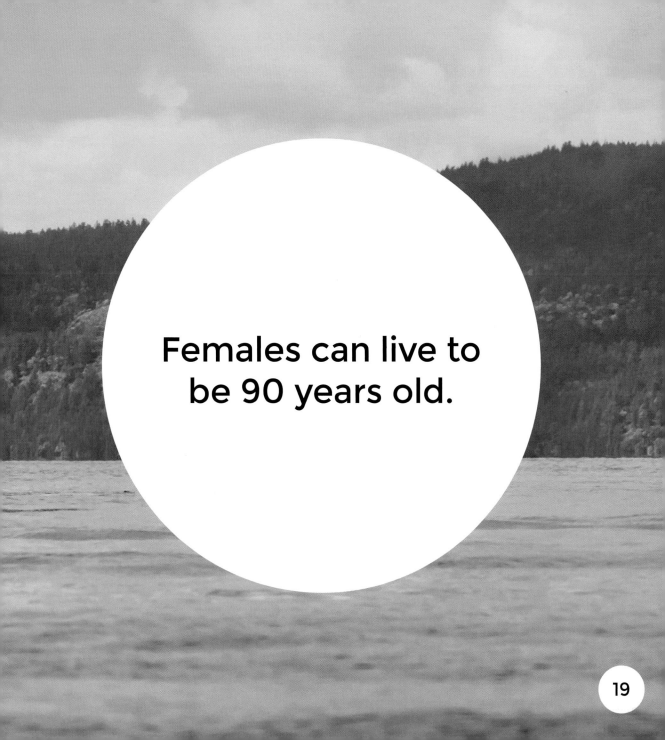

Females can live to be 90 years old.

Average Length

A killer whale is longer than a mid-size car.

25 ft   15 ft

Average Weight

A killer whale is as heavy as a delivery truck.

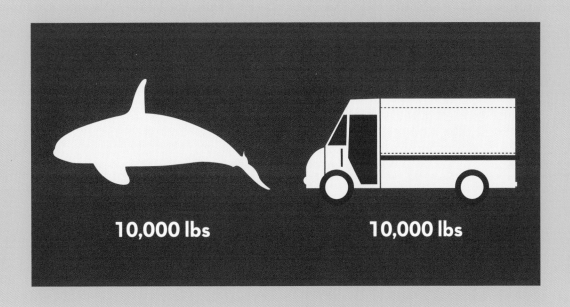

10,000 lbs   10,000 lbs

Glossary

calves - baby animals.

flippers - wide, flat limbs that sea creatures use for swimming.

melon - a rounded structure found in the forehead of some whales.

migrate - to move from one place to another, often to find food or water.

pod - a group of dolphins or whales.

prey - an animal that is hunted and eaten by another animal.

Booklinks

For more information
on **killer whales**, please visit
booklinks.abdopublishing.com

 **In on Animals!**

Learn even more with the Abdo Zoom
Animals database. Check out
abdozoom.com for more information.

Index